Prelude on

How Great Is Our God

MUSIC BY

Chris Tomlin, Jesse Reeves & Ed Cash

ARRANGED FOR SOLO PIANO BY

Timothy Shaw

worship BRIDGES

PRELUDE ON "HOW GREAT IS OUR GOD"

Music by Chris Tomlin, Jesse Reeves and Ed Cash
Arranged by TIMOTHY SHAW

13
mp
p
16
8va
8vb
8vb
19
mp
22
25
mf
rit.
mp
a tempo

rit.
p
More motion (♩ = ca. 76)
mp
r.h.
l.h.

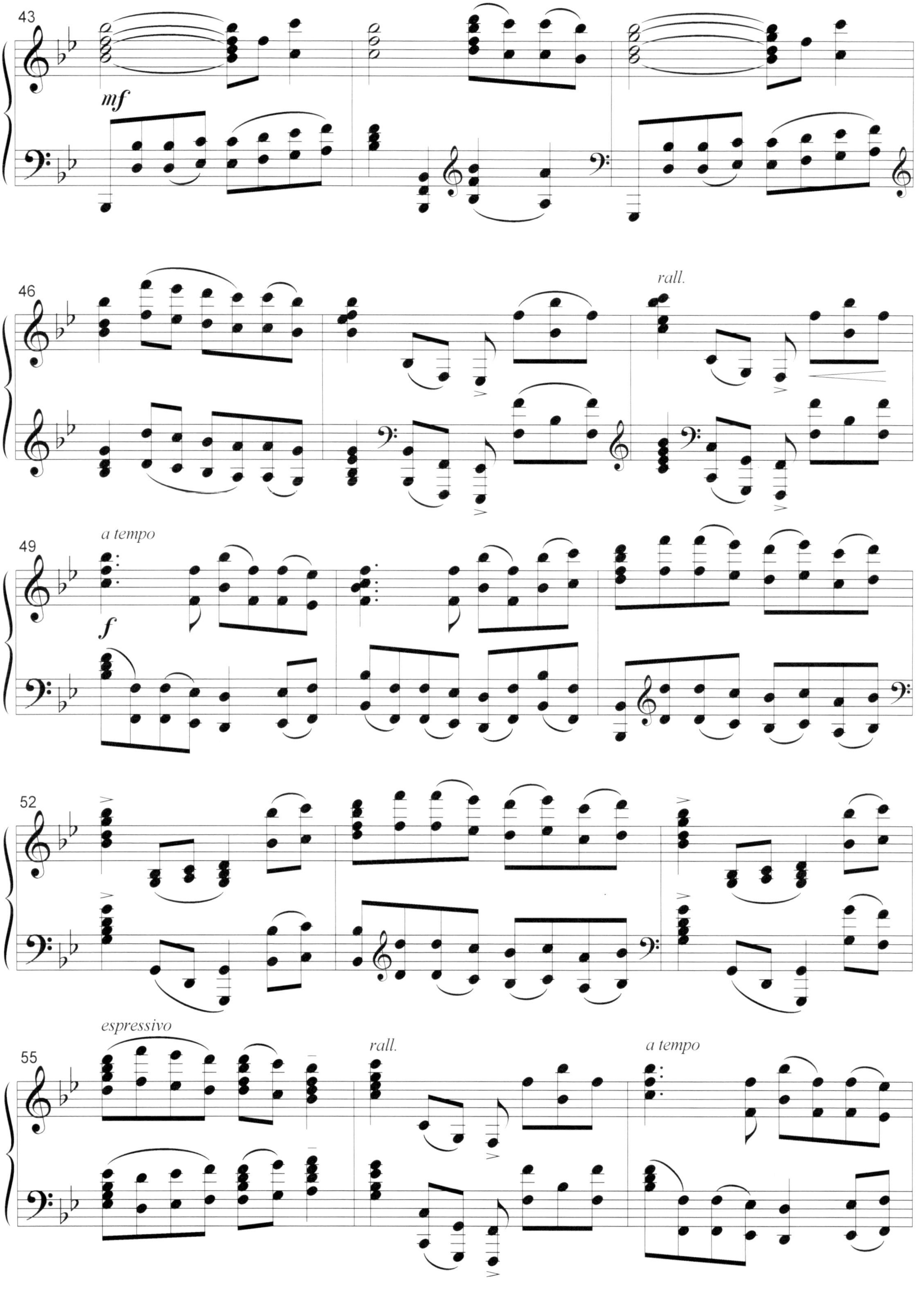
43
mf
46
rall.
49
a tempo
f
52
55
espressivo
rall.
a tempo

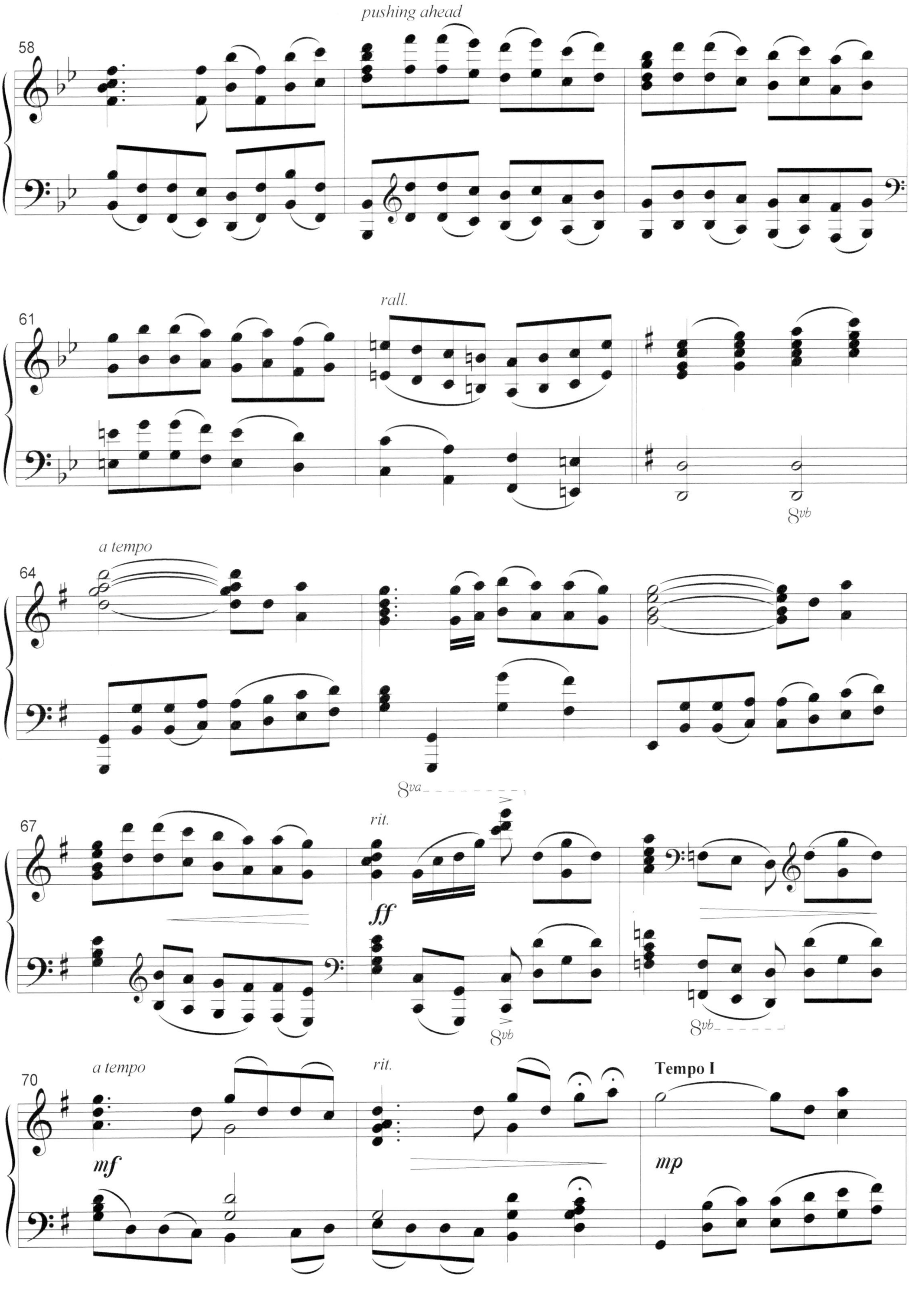
58
pushing ahead
61
rall.
8vb
64
a tempo
67
8va
rit.
ff
8vb
8vb
70
a tempo
mf
rit.
Tempo I
mp

73
76
mf
rit.
mp
a tempo
p
79
8va
8vb
rit.
82
a tempo
8va
8vb
85
8va
rit.
8va
8va
8va
pp
8vb